Original title:
Leaves That Listen

Copyright © 2025 Creative Arts Management OÜ
All rights reserved.

Author: Maya Livingston
ISBN HARDBACK: 978-1-80581-733-8
ISBN PAPERBACK: 978-1-80581-260-9
ISBN EBOOK: 978-1-80581-733-8

The Voice of the Forest's Heart

In the trees, whispers play,
Gossip of squirrels on their way.
They chuckle and chatter as they prance,
Sharing secrets in a leafy dance.

A raccoon's tale, a tale of snacks,
While rabbits plot their leafy tracks.
An acorn drops with a little thud,
Attracting ants to a munching flood.

Old oak grumbles, 'Why so loud?'
While pine needles shiver, quite proud.
The forest hums with giggles galore,
As creatures craft tales of folklore.

So next time you stroll beneath the boughs,
Listen closely, take a bow!
For every rustle is a tale untold,
In the heart of the woods, laughter unfolds.

Serenade of the Slumbering Wood

In the twilight, shadows play,
A sleepy owl thinks it's day.
He hoots out jokes, a wise old friend,
Even bushes join in, pretend.

The hedgehogs snore, a rumbling band,
Dreaming of snacks, all unplanned.
Crickets laugh as they tap their feet,
Making music to the woodland beat.

Mice dance slow, in twirling fun,
Catching moonbeams, one by one.
While sleepy trees sway with a yawn,
Their branches wave at the sleepy dawn.

So if you hear the night's soft sound,
A symphony of giggles all around.
Join the frolic, don't be shy,
In slumber's embrace, let laughter fly!

Whispers Among the Understory

In the thicket, secrets speak,
The bushes giggle, playing hide and seek.
A squirrel shares tales of acorn dreams,
While mushrooms chuckle in sun's vibrant beams.

Dancing shadows tease the ferns,
As beetles boast of wooden turns.
A wild invitation to join their spree,
Under the canopy, wild and free.

Lullabies from the Forest Floor

Beneath the boughs, a snooze so sweet,
Critters snore to a rhythmic beat.
A bunny hums to a spider's weave,
While ants march with reprieves to believe.

Daisies yawn in the gentle light,
Whispering songs of the coming night.
With every rustle, a dreamy score,
The forest sings from its cozy floor.

The Sighs of Ancient Timber

Big old trunks sway with delight,
Telling tall tales in the twilight.
A woodpecker's tap marks the fun,
As branches chuckle under the sun.

Their bark keeps secrets, oh so bright,
Of squirrel lofty and owl's flight.
In every knot, a chuckle's found,
In the wise old trees, joy does abound.

Curiosity Among the Petals

Petals blush in a breezy tease,
Rosebuds giggle at bumblebees.
A daisy whispers, 'What's the rush?'
While violets prance in an evening hush.

Butterflies flutter, their whispers loud,
In the garden, they dance, feeling proud.
With each tickle of the fragrant air,
Nature's laughter is everywhere.

Sounds of the Undergrowth

In the woods where critters peek,
Mice debate with frogs this week.
A squirrel casts a nutty joke,
While shadows giggle, and clouds poke.

A snail slips on a slippery leaf,
Declares she's late—it's a comic thief!
The acorns chuckle, tumble, and roll,
As nature's laughter takes its toll.

The Listening Heart of Nature

A tree hummed tunes in the summer sun,
While daisies danced and jumped for fun.
The wind told tales of birds and bees,
Who sighed and snorted with sneezes and wheezes.

A bear tripped over his own big paws,
Claiming it was just a round of applause.
Nature's heart tickles, overhears,
Between the chuckles and silly sneers.

Whispers in the Wilderness

In a forest filled with giggly sprites,
Crickets share secrets on starry nights.
The brook gurgles, mocks, and sings,
With fish that ponder the strangest things.

A fox plays tag with a sleepy owl,
While wise old trees shake heads and scowl.
Whispers collide with the breeze's glee,
As shrubs rearrange for the wild symphony.

Echoes of Earth and Sky

Beneath the clouds, the daisies shone,
As ants held meetings: "Who's bringing the scone?"
The echo of laughter rolled through the vale,
With grasshoppers plotting a musical tale.

A rhino snorted a tune, quite off-key,
While butterflies chuckled, sipping on tea.
The echoes of whimsy danced in the air,
As nature conspired with giggles to share.

Whispers of the Canopy

In the treetops high and bright,
Squirrels gossip through the night.
"Did you see that bird's new style?"
"Oh yes, it's been a while!"

Branches shake with fruity grins,
While woodpeckers tap for wins.
"Knock, knock; who's there?" they play,
A joke or two to sway the day.

Leaves chuckle in the breeze,
Telling tales among the trees.
"I think I saw a fox in flair!"
"With no pants? You better beware!"

Bark holds secrets dressed in bark,
"What's the buzz?" says the old lark.
"Even trees can share a laugh!"
While branches wave in a silly gaffe.

The Silent Symphony of Trees

In the forest's quiet hall,
Acorns tumble with a call.
"Hey, watch out! Don't trip!" they shout,
While raccoons nod and play about.

Frogs croak high, and crickets sing,
Nature's dance—a wobbly thing!
"Step left then right; don't miss a beat!"
The woodlands groove on leafy feet.

A deer tiptoes on fluffy moss,
Tripping lightly, what a toss!
"Can you find the hidden pine?"
"Only if I sip some wine!"

In leafy chatter, laughter spins,
As chipmunks joke about their sins.
"The nut I hid? It's in the past!"
"Just stash it safe—a squirrel's blast!"

Echoes in the Breeze

Breezy whispers dance and weave,
"What's that rustle?" They believe.
Feathered friends are in a race,
Flaunting colors—what a face!

Woodpeckers with their awesome clout,
Tap a rhythm, bring it out.
"Can you hear that buzzing sound?"
"Oh yes, the honeybees around!"

A rabbit hops, a squirrel spins,
Grinning wide, each fun begins.
"Where's the carrot? Who's the chef?"
The forest grins like no one's left.

Laughter echoes through and through,
As shadows dance 'neath skies so blue.
"What's a tree's favorite game?"
"Hide and seek—oh what a fame!"

Rustling Secrets of the Woods

In tangled vines, the stories flow,
"Did you hear? The trees all know!"
A breeze giggles, rustles leaves,
As clever ferns say their eves.

"Who took my acorn?" calls a nut,
Squirrels giggle, bark in strut.
"Don't worry friend, it's in the ground!"
"Next time, guard it like a crown!"

Sunlight dances, shadows play,
With cheeky boughs, they find a way.
"What's a forest's favorite snack?"
"Give them laughter, they'll come back!"

In the woods, a joy so bright,
Nature's jokes take flight at night.
"Wrap it up, it's time to sing!"
"A serenade from the firewing!"

The Soliloquy of the Swaying Bow

In the breeze, they dance and wave,
With secrets only they can save.
They gossip soft in rustling tones,
About the squirrels and their silly homes.

A crow sits perched, ready to jest,
While branches stretch out for a rest.
They chuckle at the passer's haste,
Slow down, friend, life's not a race!

The wind whispers, 'Guess what I found!'
A fool's acorn rolls on the ground.
Laughter echoes through and about,
As branches shake, they twist and shout!

At dusk, they share a leafy chime,
Tickling the air, oh so sublime.
When twilight falls, their stories glisten,
In the hush of night, the trees still listen.

Treetop Memorandum

A memo from the trees goes round,
'No shedding tears, just roots in the ground!'
With paper made from the finest bark,
They send out humor, with quite a spark!

Today's agenda? A gusty laugh,
Remind the ants to take the path.
No running, please! A slow parade,
We're all in this leafy escapade!

And what of clouds? They're far too shy,
Their fluff keeps slipping from the sky.
A playful poke from a twig so spry,
As drizzles turn to giggles—oh my!

So read the notes from high above,
With chuckles that the branches love.
Their grapevine tales and airy blunders,
Make merry echoes of thunderous wonders!

Silent Observers of the Seasons

They stand so still, with a cheeky stance,
Witnessing winter's clumsy dance.
Snowflakes tumble, and branches creak,
Yet in their silence, they surely speak.

Spring arrives with a playful tease,
Bud-bloomers dance in a soft breeze.
But oh, the trees roll their eyes wide,
Watching blossoms in bloom, they confide!

Summer flops in like a cat on a mat,
The branches sigh, 'Oh, imagine that!'
While shadows nap and sunbeams brawl,
Their giggles spread like a picnic call.

As autumn swirls in a crafty show,
They cackle as colors begin to glow.
Here comes a leaf, twirling with grace,
Let's catch it before it takes off in a race!

The Choir of Shifting Colors

A choir formed from shades so bright,
They warm the day and cool the night.
With reds and golds in lively tones,
Their harmonies weave through twirling drones.

The conductor, a breezy gust,
Calls forth the hues, with lively thrust.
They sway and jig, in tune they whir,
A tapestry of laughter, with a playful stir!

Here sings the orange, loud as can be,
While mellow yellows hum with glee.
The greens chime in, a jazzy tune,
Bouncing around, like a sunny balloon.

As they perform through day and night,
Their colors fade, yet spirits stay bright.
For even in rust, their laughs remain,
A world of hues—oh what a gain!

The Interlude of Emerald Light

In the park, a squirrel forgot,
The acorn he sought, that pesky little tot.
He bounced around with such flair,
Tripping over breezy air.

The sun and the grass join the play,
While shadows dance, oh what a day!
A funny frog sings a silly tune,
While butterflies dance with a swoon.

A treasure of twigs in a basket lies,
But a gust of wind plays a few tricks in disguise.
Chasing the chase, all in a flurry,
As giggles erupt without any worry.

The evening closes with a bow,
As critters gather, taking a vow.
To always remember this silly spree,
Under the sky, we'll dance with glee.

Stillness Breathing Through Green

A sleepy turtle made a mistake,
Thought he was fast but got a big shake.
He tripped over grass in a slow-motion roll,
Now he's pitched a tent in a leafy knoll.

The breeze tickles the cheeks of bold bees,
Who buzz in a rhythm, dancing with ease.
But watch out, here comes that daring hare,
Running like lightning, a fluff from the air.

Up above, a chatty sparrow winks,
While the ants wear hats and form links.
They march in a line with a grand display,
Turning the daytime into a cabaret!

As shadows stretch, the sun does boast,
Of all the laughter and silly host.
In this green realm, so fresh and spry,
We'll giggle forever, oh my, oh my!

Symphonies of the Autumnal Gale

Around the bend, a whirlwind's tune,
Swirling leaves that look like balloons.
A squirrel in socks twirls away,
While the wind whispers, "Come out and play!"

Chirping crickets play the drum,
While leaves clap along, a joyous hum.
A bunny hops, wearing a cape,
Starring in the most charming escape!

A gust of wind gives a cheeky tease,
As acorns scatter with playful ease.
The trees chuckle in rustling delight,
As nature performs its comedic sight.

With costumes of gold and fiery red,
Funny creatures dance on nature's bed.
In this humorous season of mirth,
The magic unfolds, this is nature's birth.

The Sentinels of Serenity

Two tall trees conspire and scheme,
As they share secrets like a funny dream.
With branches waving in a friendly jest,
They play hide and seek, at their leafy best.

A riddle of shadows tickles the ground,
While the wind whispers giggles all around.
A feeling of joy, without any fuss,
As squirrels form a comedic chorus.

They toss acorns in a playful jest,
Expecting the other to laugh the best.
But off they go, on a wild chase,
Frolicking with joy in this smart little race!

As twilight approaches, they hold a show,
Casting their stories for all below.
In this peaceful realm, with mischief so bright,
Serenity dances with humor in sight.

A Tale of the Watching Wood

In a grove where whispers grow,
Trees tell tales, don't you know?
Squirrels giggle up on high,
Plotting mischief in the sky.

Critters dance, a silly sight,
Mice on stilts, oh what a fright!
Bunnies hop with furry flair,
Chasing shadows, unaware.

Branches shake with muffled laughs,
Deer play poker with the staffs.
Owls wink with wisdom so bright,
Nighttime brings a wild delight.

And when the sun begins to dip,
Everyone takes a funny trip.
With giggles echoing through the trees,
Nature's playground, aim to please!

Dreaming in Shades of Green

In a meadow where dreams blend,
Caterpillars start to trend.
They wear hats and dance in line,
Sipping dew like it's fine wine.

Frogs croak out a silly tune,
Underneath the jovial moon.
Grasshoppers play leapfrog games,
While daisies tease with funny names.

Breezes tickle every bloom,
Bumblebees create a zoom.
Petals flutter like a laugh,
Nature's joy—a silly half!

So let's frolic in this dream,
Where all is funny as it seems.
In shades of green, we dance away,
Finding humor in the play!

The Echo's Embrace in Nature

In the woods where echoes sing,
The rocks and trees start arguing.
"Who's the loudest?" one does crow,
Nature giggles, don't you know?

With splashes of a stream nearby,
Fish jump up to say goodbye.
A big jump brings a splashy sound,
The trees all chuckle all around.

Bats wear capes as night draws near,
Swirling 'round with naught a fear.
They whisper secrets in the dark,
Turning shadows into lark.

Amidst the echoes, laughter flows,
And even flowers strike a pose.
Such a scene—oh what a chase!
Nature's joy—a comical place!

In the Realm of Pattering Rain

In a realm where raindrops play,
Clouds hold contests every day.
"Who can make the biggest splash?"
They giggle loud, it's quite a bash!

Puddles form a dance floor wide,
Worms in tuxedos slide and glide.
While misty gnomes begin to cheer,
Jolly sounds fill the dampened sphere.

A rabbit jumps, a splashy scene,
Dancing 'round in shades of green.
Frogs with umbrellas join the fun,
As rainbow-banded skies are spun.

And when the rain starts to decline,
Sunbeams peek through, expansion divine.
Nature's laugh, all wet but bright,
Brings joy and giggles in the light!

Conversations Between the Shadows

In the twilight, shadows play,
They gossip about the day.
One says, 'Did you see that cat?'
The other replies, 'No, but I heard the splat!'

In the breeze, they share a joke,
A ticklish breeze, a playful poke.
'Why do trees always stand so tall?'
'Because they're too shy to go to the ball!'

They chuckle as the night creeps in,
Under the stars, they spin and grin.
Whispers float from bush to glade,
While fireflies join the parade!

A spook and a laugh, the moon aloof,
Shadows blend in leafy proof.
What fun it is to talk so sly,
In the dark where mischief flies!

The Pulse Beneath the Bark

Under the trunk, there's a hum,
A secret beat, a woodland drum.
The saplings sway with joyful glee,
'The heartbeat's here! Come dance with me!'

Minerals argue, 'I'm the best!'
The tree grins wide, 'You're all my guests!'
Roots jiggle in a funky way,
As critters laugh and join the fray.

'What's that? A squirrel on the prowl!'
'No, it's just Gus! He's on the growl!'
Bark rolls its eyes at rhythmic prance,
'Enough of this! Let's start a dance!'

With every pulse, new tales unfold,
In the wood, adventures told.
Life thrums bright, so wild and stark,
In the laughter found beneath the bark!

Echoes of the Hidden Realm

In the thicket, whispers spark,
Echoes play from dawn till dark.
A bumblebee's got quite a tale,
Of how he outsmarted a gusty gale!

The mushrooms giggle on the floor,
'Did you hear the tree's loud snore?'
As branches sway, they start to tease,
'C'mon now, join us, swing with ease!'

Frogs croak symphonies, quite absurd,
A toad joins in, spreading the word.
'When the moon is high, we leap and sing,
It's a party! Come dance, it's a lovely thing!'

In this grove, mirth overflows,
Where laughter blooms and fun just grows.
Echoes ring and tales arise,
In the hidden realm, laughter flies!

Nature's Whispered Memories

Breezes tell of days gone by,
When bears wore hats and danced on high.
Trees stored secrets in their rings,
Of joyous antics and silly things.

A chipmunk's cheeky smile is bright,
He hoards his nuts with all his might.
'Remember when the owl tripped, oh my!'
The forest roars with a hearty sigh.

Mushrooms boast of where they've been,
How they've danced on raindrops, oh so keen.
'The hydrant blooms were quite a site,'
Nature giggles at the memory's height.

In the twilight glow, stories blend,
Nature shares with a wink and a mend.
Every whisper is a chance to see,
The humor wrapped in earth's decree!

Soft Songs of the Woodland

In the woods where whispers play,
Squirrels chatter, what a day!
Trees hum tunes, a leafy band,
Nature's music, oh so grand!

Twirling dancers, bark on toes,
Raccoons giggle, what a show!
The wildflowers sway in time,
To the rhythm, oh so prime!

Fungi croon a mushroom beat,
While mosquitos tap their feet.
Bees bring honey, sweet and bright,
All join in, what a delight!

A chipmunk's laugh, a joyous snort,
Even crickets hold a court!
Every branch and rustling leaf,
Can't help but bring you such relief!

The Quiet Observers

In the garden, secrets hide,
Worms gossip, oh what pride!
Ants parade, a tiny line,
Counting steps, they tow the line.

Butterflies with painted wings,
Critique the ants and their things.
Beetles spin tales in the dirt,
Whispering jokes, while not pert.

A fox sneezes, fashion faux pas,
Hiding laughs, like a big star!
Nature giggles, quiet at best,
In silent chuckles, they invest!

Night owls hoot with sass and flair,
Challenging shadows with a glare.
The moon chuckles, lighting the way,
Inviting all to join the fray!

Shades of Memory and Wind

The breeze tickles through the trees,
Sharing tales of flying bees.
Memories swirl in a playful dance,
Fluffy clouds in a trance.

Swaying branches, nodding heads,
Whispering dreams upon their beds.
A wise old owl in a nearby nook,
Reading laughter from a book.

The dandelion lifts a grin,
Blown away, it's far from thin.
Jumping seeds on a merry flight,
Sprinkling joy in the warm sunlight.

The pines chuckle, tall and neat,
As rabbits dance with tiny feet.
Nature's canvas, fun and bright,
Drawing smiles both day and night!

Telltale Green

The grass whispers secrets low,
Giggles spin where wild things grow.
Each twig wears a little grin,
As the breeze whispers soft within.

Dandelions, gold and bold,
Tell stories of the brave and old.
Sunflowers nod, up to the sky,
Winking at the clouds passing by.

Frogs in croaks, a comic play,
Sing of dreams that jump and sway.
As shadows prance on the ground,
Nature's humor knows no bound!

With every rustle, every crease,
The world wraps laughter, wild and free.
Join the fun, it's pure delight,
In the green of day and night!

Stories Carried on the Wind

The breeze whispers tales to the trees,
Of squirrels that dance and tease.
A chipmunk juggles with acorns so round,
While the robin sings of a cat that's found.

The wind carries giggles, oh what a hoot,
As branches sway, they claim their loot.
A pinecone plops on a crow's silly head,
"Oh no!" caws the bird, "not my style!" he said.

With rustling tales, they share their jests,
Of critters that wear mismatched vests.
A worm in a top hat, a snail in a tie,
Their fashion choices make even trees sigh.

So listen close to the rustling cheer,
The wind's gossip carries far and near.
Under the canopy, there's always a plot,
Of acrobatic antics that never get caught.

The Poetry of Shimmering Canopies

In a world where shadows boast and play,
A beetle's reciting rhymes all day.
With a twirl and a flip, it stumbles so sweet,
The sun snaps a picture of its tiny feet.

Up high, the leaves giggle, soaking the sun,
"Don't miss this, the party is just begun!"
A butterfly flutters, wearing a grin,
While ants form a conga line, wiggling in.

Through the branches, a squirrel tells a tale,
Of acorn heists that always prevail.
It's a comedy show with a slapstick twist,
As each little critter adds to the list.

A raccoon raps about midnight snacks,
While crickets drop beats, giving all they've got.
The trees hold their breath, all gathered around,
As nature's funny poetry knows no bound.

Tales of the Twilight Thicket

In twilight's glow, secrets get spun,
A hedgehog sneezes, "Oh, that's no fun!"
With a leaf for a tissue, it tries to be neat,
But the other critters just collapse in their seat.

The fireflies flicker, creating a scene,
As frogs in tuxedos leap and careen.
Their croaks turn to songs, a chorus so loud,
"Where's the dinner?" they yell, feeling proud.

The moon joins the jest, a spotlight at last,
As shadows break out in a wild, quirky cast.
There's a raccoon called Ricky, who juggles some snails,
While an owl hoots rhythm, flapping its sails.

So gather 'round, all you woodland folks,
In the thicket of twilight, laughter invokes.
With every prank pulled and every jest told,
The night's thick with stories, both silly and bold.

Soundtrack of the Saplings

In a grove where the saplings sway with a grin,
The wind tunes up; let the fun begin!
With rustles and whispers that tickle the air,
Tiny saplings sway, with jokes to share.

Each branch has a solo, a rhythm to tease,
As squirrels join in, setting hearts at ease.
Their chatter a symphony, so spirited and bright,
Playing nature's hits, oh what a delight!

The grass joins the melody, humming along,
While bees beat the drums, buzzing their song.
With giggles and grins, they dance on the ground,
Creating a ballet that's magic profound.

In this orchestra of greenery, fun takes its flight,
With chuckles and chirps from morning till night.
So listen intently, and you'll surely find,
The music of nature is playful and kind.

Nature's Written Memoirs

In the breeze, they whisper tales,
Of squirrels' antics and their fails.
Each rustle hints of gossip rife,
A comedy in the wild, full of life.

They giggle as the robins flirt,
While ants march on, all covered in dirt.
A bumblebee steals a dance or two,
While the sun sets in a golden hue.

Old owls wink with a knowing glance,
As crickets plot their evening dance.
The stories weave, a joyous sound,
In nature's book where laughter's found.

So when you stroll beneath the sky,
Listen close, give it a try.
For in the rustle, jokes abound,
In nature's memoirs, humor's found.

The Heartbeat of the Forest

In the woods, where shadows play,
Trees chuckle in their own way.
With every breeze that shakes the boughs,
Funny faces, it seems, they've found.

A woodpecker beats a silly tune,
While chipmunks dance beneath the moon.
The pine trees sway, they lean and bow,
As if to say, "We're judging how!"

The forest floor's a comedy stage,
Where every critter is a sage.
With a flick of a tail, the opossum grins,
And the laughter of the woodland spins.

So, next time you wander through the green,
Look for the fun that lies unseen.
For in each thump and every creak,
The woods have jokes they love to speak.

Rhapsodies of the Green Home

In a garden where the daisies dance,
Wrens enact their comic prance.
With petals bright and colors bold,
Stories of the bees are humorously told.

Beetles roll their little balls,
While hedge pigs dart and have their brawls.
The worms all squiggle, sharing their bliss,
While the cat sneaks in for a sudden kiss.

The cucumber vines, they laugh and twist,
As the pepper shrugs, "I'm not on the list!"
Such rhapsodies in nature's space,
A garden giggle, a cheerful place.

So if you pause by the little blooms,
You'll hear the laughter, dispelling glooms.
In every corner, joy does roam,
In nature's choir, they call it home.

The Hushed Conversations

In the twilight where shadows creep,
The flora gossip, but don't make a peep.
With a flutter, the petals share,
Secrets wrapped in the fragrant air.

The daisies sigh with tales of bees,
While the thorns chuckle at tragic pleas.
A shy fern whispers with delight,
"Last night's rain was quite a sight!"

The vines loop close, sharing their dreams,
As the mist rolls in with giggly schemes.
Caught in whispers of dusk's embrace,
Nature's humor weaves a gentle lace.

So lean in closer, let your heart liven,
For in the hush, the joy is given.
Listen well to the trees' soft posture,
In the mute symphony, find laughter's texture.

Secrets Woven in Green

In the garden, whispers play,
Tiny voices laugh each day.
Rustling tales of silly things,
A dance of joy that nature brings.

Petals giggle in the breeze,
Tickling ants upon their knees.
Rabbits share their secret snacks,
While the frogs make quacking whacks.

The sun smirks down from the sky,
As clouds float by with a sigh.
Each raindrop has a story spun,
Of puddle splashes—oh, such fun!

With every rustle, every cheer,
The world's so funny, crystal clear.
In hues of green, their jokes unfold,
Nature's laughter, a treasure of gold.

The Dialogue of Seasons

Winter flirts with summer's heat,
While fall's in boots, taps its feet.
Spring giggles as flowers tease,
Creating chaos with such ease.

"Your snowflakes are just frosty sighs!"
Claims warm sun with radiant eyes.
"I bring the bloom, the colors bright!"
Pouts winter back, "I own the night!"

They banter on, a feathery jest,
Swapping jokes, each one the best.
Nature's chat, a funny wrangle,
How each season starts to dangle.

Yet in the laughter, cycles flow,
Together they put on a show.
With quips and quacks, they spin their tale,
In the dance of life, they never fail.

Beneath the Shade of Understanding

Under shading arms of green,
Whispers float, a funny scene.
"Why don't you ever wear a hat?"
A sunflower quips, feeling sprat.

"I'd look quite silly, what about you?"
Said the oak tree with a view.
"I'm just too tall for any shade,
But I can lend some, I'm well-made!"

The wind chuckles, swaying low,
"Both of you, just go with flow!"
And so they chat, a friendly brawl,
In shades of green, they share it all.

With laughter echoing in the air,
Nature's jokes without a care.
Beneath the branches, banter sings,
Life is funny in leafy rings.

Harmony Among the Foliage

In the thicket, fun prevails,
With leafy tales and froggy wails.
Squirrels dart, a cheeky race,
While daisies giggle in their place.

"Why so serious?" the vines proclaim,
"Join our game, no need for fame!"
The bushes snicker, swinging wide,
As butterflies take joyride.

Beneath the trunks, the shade does hum,
A squirrel dance, a lovely thrum.
Every branch, a comedic branch-out,
Nature's harmony, without a doubt.

The rustling crowd shares jokes so grand,
In this leafy, vibrant band.
Among the foliage, laughter flows,
A symphony of funny shows.

The Unheard Breezes

In the forest, whispers sway,
That chuckle in daylight's play.
Silly sounds from branches tall,
While squirrels giggle, having a ball.

The willows sway with glee,
As they tell jokes in harmony.
A breeze tickles the bugs in flight,
While ants dance in pure delight.

The rustling jokes, a mystery,
What secrets lie in that old tree?
The wind is a comedian, it seems,
Making fun of all our dreams.

So next time you wander by,
Don't forget to stop and sigh.
For in the air, humor's spun,
In nature's laughter, we are one.

Emblems of Silent Thought

In quiet woods, where shadows play,
A bush reveals a joke or two today.
The flowers giggle, petals bright,
While bushes snicker in the light.

A mushroom grins beneath the sun,
As if it knows just how to pun.
The grass is tickled by tiny feet,
While daisies dance to a funny beat.

A fox walks by, all suave and sly,
While trees shake branches in reply.
Every twig has its own sense of fun,
Here's a riddle to share with the sun!

Oh, the silence hides a lively jest,
Where nature's humor is manifest.
Listen closely, hear the cheer,
For secrets of laughter linger near.

The Sentient Glade

In a glade where shadows prance,
A frog plays tunes, what a chance!
The crickets chirp a rhythm sweet,
While rabbits jump to the lively beat.

Beneath the oaks, stories unfold,
As chipmunks chat, and chatter bold.
A breeze brushes past with a wink,
While wise old owls just stop and think.

Giggling streams with wise remarks,
Swaying flowers, planting sparks.
In every nook, a joke's brewed rare,
Nature's business, beyond compare.

So if you stroll through leafy veins,
And hear the laughter in the rains,
Just smile wide and join the fun,
Nature's humor has just begun.

Echoing Rhythms of Green

Bamboos sway like they're in a groove,
As if they're dancing, trying to move.
The ferns are tapping in leafy shoes,
While flowers bloom in bold, bright hues.

Every rustle holds a playful jest,
As insects gather, they're quite the fest!
With pretty petals flapping away,
The trees all nod, as if to say:

'Join the rhythm, sway along!'
Where every sound sings nature's song.
With chuckles echoing through the grove,
This verdant realm is laughter's trove.

So roam beneath the vibrant scene,
And catch the sight of every green.
For in the laughter of this play,
Nature smiles and leads the way.

Echoes of the Verdant Realm

In a dance of green, they sway in glee,
The whispers of nature, wild and free.
They giggle and chatter, oh what a spree,
Telling tales of the wind and the bumblebee.

A squirrel, in a costumed getup, pranced,
His acorn hat on, he fancied a dance.
With every twist, he took a chance,
While branches chuckled, caught in a trance.

"Hey, I saw you fall!" a twig would shout,
"Next time, aim for the clouds, not a rout!"
Leaves snicker softly, without a doubt,
As nature's jesters make the whole world sprout.

In this realm of green, where joy is the goal,
The rustling foliage plays a merry role.
Each quip and quirk makes the forest whole,
With whispers and laughter, it captures the soul.

The Language of Branches

Branches chatter in the sun's warm glow,
While squirrels retell the gossip they know.
A raccoon pipes up, with a wink and a show,
    As everyone listens to tales of woe.

"Did you hear," said one, "that acorn fell flat?"
"Oh please," replies another, "was he wearing a hat?"
With every turn, there's a humorous spat,
    As nature's own jesters engage in chit-chat.

The shadows giggle, the sunlight beams bright,
As ferns flap their fronds in sheer delight.
"Who knew staying still could feel so right?"
    In this leafy circus, all is light and slight.

So dance, dear branches, and share your delight,
In the laughter of greens, take wing and take flight.
In the whispers of wind, you'll find pure insight,
    A funny family, forever in sight.

Chronicles of the Green Canopy

Beneath the boughs, stories unfold,
Of conquests by critters, both timid and bold.
A snail claims the throne, "I'm fast," he's told,
While the dawn's early light brings laughter untold.

A fluttering butterfly flits by in style,
"Did you see that move? Was that worth the while?"
The leaves clap their hands and giggle a mile,
Each motion a story, each turn a good smile.

"Let's play hide and seek," a brave leaf proposes,
And soon every branch has a new set of poses.
The laughter erupts as the game discloses,
That nature's a prankster, and so many knowses.

In this green world, full of whimsy and cheer,
Every rustling whisper brings joy near.
With tales that frolic, the skies feel clear,
Chronicles woven, from far and from near.

Murmurs Beneath the Boughs

Beneath the boughs where the shadows play,
Whispers of mischief unfold every day.
The ferns raise their eyebrows, while crickets relay,
Stories of folly that never decay.

"Oh, can you believe?" said a sly little sprout,
"A hedgehog tried dancing, but fell on his snout!"
Laughter erupts, as all joke about,
This forest of jesters makes chaos a rout.

A wise old owl hoots, "Gather 'round, friends!"
He spins out a tale that twists and bends.
As giggles take flight, the mirth never ends,
With every quip, the joy transcends.

So linger a while, with nature's own crew,
Where humor abounds and the laughter is true.
Beneath every bough lies something askew,
In this magical world, where nonsense renews.

The Language of Dappled Light

Under sunlit whispers, they dance bright,
A cheeky waltz in the golden sight,
Each flutter and swirl, a giggle of glee,
Telling secrets to squirrels, oh what a spree!

Beneath the branches, shadows play tag,
As sunlight pranks, feeling quite brash,
The beams slip through, with a glimmering nudge,
Making even the grumpiest trees give a smudge.

Rustling confetti, a breeze starts to sway,
Tickling the trunks in a playful ballet,
Nature's own comic, with jokes to unwind,
Cracking up silence, it's all quite unkind!

So here in the dappled, where fun's never slight,
The chatter of foliage brings pure delight,
For each giggle shared, a smile to ignite,
In the language of wonder—it's all just right!

Choreography of the Forest Floor

On the soft stage, where mushrooms grow,
The ants in tuxedos put on quite a show,
With twirls and leaps, they scurry about,
Even the toadstools are dancing, no doubt!

A raccoon prances with a belly full of cheer,
While the hedgehogs on drums make their music clear,
The fox, with flair, leads the whole parade,
As the owls clap hands in the shade!

Acorns roll, a slippery prank,
Creating a laugh as they spin and clank,
The mat of leaves gets in on the fun,
While the sunbeams join, and the laughter runs!

In this wild ballet of nature's delight,
Every tiniest critter shares the spotlight,
Twirling and leaping with joy all around,
In the choreography of earth, silliness found!

The Wisdom of Verdant Silence

In stillness resides the sage old trees,
Whispering tales to the fickle breeze,
With grumpy gnarls and a stoic air,
Their wisdom is lost, or so it may appear.

Yet listen closely, hear the chuckle,
As the wise roots grumble and the branches shuffle,
With thoughts of sap and tall tales of shade,
Their humor is ripe; you just need to wade!

A ponderous pause, then a sudden whoosh,
A burly bear stumbles, "Oh, I need a push!"
While the ferns giggle, spreading tales far and wide,
Of the wise in the green, who just can't hide!

So here's to the silence, a sweet kind of jest,
A trickster's heart at nature's behest,
For wisdom's not just in the hush of the night,
But in giggles and snorts of unfiltered delight!

Soft Anthems of Autumn

As autumn tiptoes with a whimsical flair,
Colors ignite like a bold, fancy fair,
With leaves in a frolic, a jazzy display,
Even the wind can't help but sway!

The squirrels exchange their nutty goodbyes,
With chortles and giggles, they plot their replies,
In a cloak of confusion, they scamper and hop,
While trees laugh along, "Don't fall! Don't drop!"

Crispness in air gives a winky surprise,
As crunchy confetti flits up to the skies,
Each rustle a melody, a soft serenade,
An anthem of laughter in nature made!

So gather round, for the fall festival fun,
With silly faced pumpkins and mischief begun,
In the soft autumn air, it's all jolly and bright,
Where every leaf dances, a sheer delight!

Conversations Under the Trees

Beneath the branches, whispers fly,
Squirrels converse, as the birds pass by.
"Did you hear the owl? He's quite the flirt!"
"Oh please, he's just after my nutty dessert!"

The breeze is chuckling, as shadows prance,
While cheeky raccoons plot their romance.
"I'll steal his acorn, then you steal his hat!"
"No way! It's my turn; you just stole the cat!"

The Wisdom of Fall's Embrace

The wise old tree has tales to tell,
About sleepy bears and where they fell.
"Did you see that chipmunk dance in a whirl?"
"Yes, I thought he'd audition for a twirling girl!"

Leaves in jackets, colors so bright,
Debating who's best dressed in the sunlight.
"I've got oranges, you've got bright reds!"
"Still, that gold one's the real head of threads!"

Whirling Secrets in the Breeze

A flick of the wrist, how fast they spin,
The wind tells secrets where giggles begin.
"That ladybug's wearing a polka-dot tie!"
"No way! I think he's just aiming to fly!"

Dandelions whisper, in puffs of delight,
"Have you heard? The toads are planning tonight!"
"What's on the agenda? A dance at the pond?"
"Nope, just a nap—s'like, come on, respond!"

The Eavesdropping Grove

In the grove, secrets tickle the leaves,
While old branches giggle, it's all in their sleeves.
"Did you hear the rabbit hope for a meal?"
"He's on a diet! What's the deal?"

The blooms nod their heads in green mimicry,
As cicadas complain about the heat's misery.
"Can you believe we've got to just sit?"
"They should renew our membership—it's quite a fit!"

The Unseen Choir of Canopies

In the forest where the shadows play,
Beneath the branches, a tune's on display.
Squirrels are drumming, and birds do sing,
While beetles are buzzing, doing their thing.

Tiny ants march in perfect time,
Chasing each other, like a silly mime.
The sunbeams dance, a spotlight bright,
On this concert of whimsy, pure delight.

A raccoon steals snacks, a true gourmand,
While rabbits hop, giving music a hand.
With nature grooving in splendid array,
Their laughter and mischief steal the day.

So if you listen with an open heart,
You'll hear the giggles of nature's smart art.
A choir unseen, but always near,
In the thrumming green, hilarity's clear.

The Secretive Art of Thicket

In the thicket where secrets unfold,
Gossiping vines share stories untold.
A fence post leans in with a wink,
As wise old ferns giggle and think.

Dandelions plot, with their fluffy heads,
Fuming over wishes that once were said.
Rabbits engage in a humorous race,
While shadows play tag, putting smiles on the face.

The bushes are chuckling, wise in their ways,
As the sun sets lower, ending the days.
With whispers so sneaky, they craft their art,
In a world full of mirth, it's a lively part.

So next time you wander, don't keep it tight,
Join in the fun, feel the delight.
The thicket may hide a joke or two,
Through leaves and twigs, laughter shines through.

Poetic Whispers from Above

Branches sway in a gentle breeze,
Sharing verses with the buzzing bees.
Clouds float by, rolling in fits of cheer,
As they snicker softly, just out of ear.

A wise old owl gives a knowing hoot,
While crickets chirp in their best little suit.
The wind carries tales from high above,
Of bumblebee blunders and butterflies in love.

Raindrops dribble like laughter around,
A splash of humor, it knows no bound.
These poetic whispers, a sweet serenade,
In the canopy realm, where nature's displayed.

So glance at the sky and hear their song,
In the playful notes, where hearts belong.
For nature crafts verses of giggles and glee,
If you stop and listen, oh, what a spree!

The Cadence of Shifting Colors

In autumn's flair, colors twist and shout,
Crimson shout 'Look!', while gold gives a pout.
The trees put on a flamboyant show,
As if they're saying, 'Watch us glow!'

With solemn greens embracing the change,
And dancing oranges appearing quite strange.
Leaves trot around, a parade quite absurd,
With every gust, they just feel so stirred.

A leaf takes a tumble, oh won't it land?
Jumping like children in a bouncy band.
With giggles aplenty, in this hue galore,
The dance of the colors, who could ask for more?

So waltz through the woods, and join the spree,
Where colors converge, so wild and free.
In this festive whirlwind, jump, clap, and cheer,
For the magical colors are always near.

Verdant Secrets in Twilight

In the trees where whispers play,
Squirrels gossip night and day.
"Who stole my acorn?" one will shout,
While birds just giggle, running out.

Frogs croak tunes, a comical band,
Dancing shadows on the land.
They leap and splash with such delight,
Making echoes in the night.

A breeze brings laughter, soft and light,
Crickets chirp in sheer delight.
"Did you hear that?" one leaf will tease,
As insects sway and hum with ease.

Beneath the sky, they have their say,
Jokes flow freely, come what may.
With nature's chuckles everywhere,
Twilight holds its funny flair.

Harmonics of Nature's Archive

In the woods, a song unfolds,
As ancient tales are lightly told.
Mice giggle at an owl's surprise,
"Who knew wisdom had such big eyes?"

Busy ants march in a line,
Underneath the moon's soft shine.
"Excuse us, friends, we're on a quest,
To find the crumbs we know the best!"

With each breeze, a rustled cheer,
Trees swapping secrets, loud and clear.
"A frog just hiccuped!" one bark sighed,
"Might be the frogs who're trying to hide!"

The night hums sweet, a lively muse,
In nature's choir, there's no excuse.
Laughter dances, echoes wide,
With the harmony of leafy pride.

When Nature Strikes a Chord

A branch hits a joke on the low,
"I'm just here to steal the show!"
With roots that chuckle, deep and low,
As flowers sway with a bright glow.

Crickets strum their tiny strings,
Announcing secrets the forest brings.
"Shh, don't tell a soul," says one,
While beetles hide, they think it's fun.

Breezes tease with a gentle stroke,
"Hey tree, what's that old oak joke?"
"Why don't we ever get a call?
Because we always drop the ball!"

The night is bright with playful sounds,
As nature's laughter wraps the grounds.
In every signal, life invites,
Funny business in the twilight nights.

The Unseen Dialogues

In rustling whispers, secrets fly,
Behind each rustle, a giggle, oh my!
"Did you see that?" a twig mentions,
While snails share their slow intentions.

Beneath the sky, they trade their puns,
Poking fun at the rising suns.
"Too bright for us," the shadows say,
As rabbits munch their grass buffet.

Butterflies swap their best moves,
Creating chaos as nature grooves.
"Catch me if you can!" they cry,
While frogs leap laughs, oh my, oh my!

As the moon rises, they take a rest,
Dreaming of jokes they know the best.
In the dark, the magic spins,
Where unseen dialogues bring the grins.

Hidden Narratives of the Grove

In the forest, whispers fly,
With squirrels acting like spies.
Trees giggle at the gossip,
As acorns roll with a plop.

A bird sings a tune so sweet,
While ants tap-dance on the route to greet.
Bugs wear hats made of dew,
In their own grand masquerade crew.

Moss jokes about its fuzzy beard,
How many hugs it has endeared!
Twigs tangle in laughter and fun,
As shadows play from sun to sun.

Nature's comedy unfolds with ease,
Creating giggles in the breeze.
With each photon, the stories grow,
Under the trees, the hilarity flows.

A Conversation with Earth's Breath

The wind tells tales between the trees,
Of lost socks and buzzing bees.
Each gust a message, a silly jest,
As blossoms sway in floral fest.

Grass blades stretch as they yawn,
Sharing secrets at the break of dawn.
The worms joke about being bent,
While snails count their slow descent.

Bees debate who's the best dancer,
While pollen twirls like a prancing prancer.
Frogs croak out their morning cue,
A chorus of ribbits, all anew.

In this concert of nature's glee,
Every rustle is full of esprit.
As Earth's breath takes center stage,
Funny stories fill every page.

The Hush of Sunlit Canopies

Under canopies, shadows play,
A squirrel mimics in a funny way.
Sunbeams tickle at branches high,
As giggles escape from the sky.

A lizard sunbathes with grand flair,
Ignoring the flies buzzing with care.
The vines tease with a twist and a turn,
While daisies bloom, a laugh they churn.

The breeze whistles a goofy tune,
As butterflies prance like a cartoon.
Each petal sways with light-hearted cheer,
Spreading joy far and near.

Underneath the playful hues,
Nature's comedy always ensues.
In the hush, if you lend an ear,
You might catch a chuckle, a giggle, or cheer.

Amity in the Arboreal Realm

In the woods where friendships blend,
Trees high-five around the bend.
Saplings giggle in a playful clump,
As critters leap and thump.

The owls share wisdom with a wink,
While mushrooms cause folks to think.
A raccoon's antics, a comedic dance,
Make even the weary take a chance.

The foxes play hide and seek,
Amidst laughter and friendly peaks.
Every nook hides a charming scene,
With antics that are quite routine.

In this realm of light and shade,
Every jest and laugh is made.
Together in this merry game,
In the woods, it's all the same.

The Gentle Cadences of Nature

The trees gossip softly, in whispers so light,
As squirrels dance around, a silly delight.
Birds drop their tunes, like confetti from skies,
Nature's own comedy, a play full of sighs.

The flowers hold meetings, they chuckle and beam,
With petals all fluttering, caught up in a dream.
The sunbeams eavesdrop on secrets so rare,
While daisies just giggle, without a single care.

Breezes play tug-of-war, branches sway in jest,
Nature's own laughter, a well-woven quest.
Amidst the green shadows, the stories unfold,
In the hearty chorus, the truth we behold.

A crunch of fallen twigs, a joke shared too loud,
As wise old oaks chuckle, their barks feeling proud.
In this wacky wonder, life dances in time,
With humor and joy, nature's genuine rhyme.

Beneath the Thicket's Gaze

In the thicket, a squirrel spreads tales of its feast,
While mushrooms discuss how to lure in a beast.
The shrubs shake with giggles, they blush deep in green,
With every soft rustle, a prank yet unseen.

A butterfly flutters, 'What's that on your face?'
A ladybug answers, 'Just my fashionable grace!'
The frogs croak in rhythm, rapping all night,
As the stars turn to chuckles, shining so bright.

The tall grass waves hello, a quick dance of glee,
While hedgehogs gossip, 'Did you see that old bee?'
With nonsense and chuckles, the wild life thrives,
Beneath the thicket's gaze, pure laughter survives.

The porcupines ponder, but not for too long,
As each little rustle joins in the song.
A symphony of mischief, hidden and grand,
Underneath the thicket, where wonders expand.

The Sound of Green Dreams

Every morning dew drop plays a tiny note,
While ants march in rhythm, all in a big coat.
Caterpillars twirl, doing pirouettes bright,
As the whispers of grass tickle bugs in delight.

A fruit bat giggles, 'What'll I munch next?'
While crickets debate who's the funniest pest.
The sunflowers nod, their humor's so grand,
As shadows keep secrets, hand-in-hand.

Here in the wild, reality plays tricks,
Pinecones report news, a heckler's quick flicks.
The breeze takes a bow, it's the coziest show,
Where laughter abounds – in a green undertow.

And as the sun sets, all creatures unwind,
In this musical patch, pure fun you will find.
The sound of green dreams, a carousel spin,
Where every little giggle begins once again.

A Symphony of Rustling Voices

Rustling leaves have secrets, they giggle and jest,
A chorus of whispers that never find rest.
Through branches they sashay, a dance of delight,
In the symphony's embrace, they float through the night.

The grass swings and sways, tickling toes in the breeze,
While chipmunks play tag, climbing high in the trees.
A raccoon tells stories, they're wild and absurd,
As the wind steals a joke, but not a word heard.

The rhythm of life hums, a tune so unique,
Where the daisies gossip, and the willows all peek.
Every swirl of the air carries snickers and fun,
In this rustic orchestra, laughter's never done.

With each flicker of light, shadows dance in the glade,
And the owls drop punchlines, in the evening parade.
In this symphony joyful, where nature delights,
We find the wild laughter that echoes through nights.

Nature's Quiet Chronicle

In the woods where squirrels creep,
The trees have secrets that they keep.
They giggle as the ripples rise,
And gossip through their leafy ties.

A breeze will shake an acorn loose,
The chatter starts, with great deduce.
"Did you see that critter fall?"
Laughter echoes down the hall.

From tree to tree, the stories flow,
Of falling branches and dodging snow.
The woodpecker's tap is the beat,
To nature's tune, oh so sweet!

With every rustle, there's a jest,
In the arboreal comedy fest.
A chorus of chuckles fills the air,
As nature's jesters lay their glare.

Whispers in the Canopy

Up above, a squirrel twirls,
While leaves drop down in playful swirls.
"Did you bring snacks?" a crow will jest,
As nature giggles, feeling blessed.

Branches wave like arms in glee,
The sun dips low—they're free as can be!
With each whisper of the breeze,
A chuckle flows through all the trees.

The tadpoles giggle in the pond,
As frogs jump high and then respond.
They ribbit jokes, a ribald show,
While bullfrogs croak, "You're too slow!"

In shadows deep, the banter swings,
As owls hoot tales of wondrous things.
Beneath the stars, with twinkling light,
The canopy laughs into the night.

Secrets of the Rustling Foliage

The branches creak with tales of fun,
As breezes dance beneath the sun.
The willow sways and winks an eye,
"Don't look now, a bird just flew by!"

Beneath the shade, the insects cheer,
As beetles march—no time for fear.
"Who knew we'd host this wild parade?"
The flowers smile, all colors displayed.

They share the quirks of farmers' hats,
And laugh at birds who chase their bats.
"Last week, a raccoon tried to peek!"
The leaves erupt with whispered squeaks.

The tales of nature, oh so sly,
Keep us giggling as time flies by.
In every rustle, there's delight,
A merry comedy in the night.

Nature's Silent Confidants

In the stillness, secrets reign,
A tree might chuckle—it's all in vain.
"Did you hear? That rabbit's late!"
The ferns giggle, sharing fate.

The dandelions puff and sway,
Blowing whispers that drift away.
"Watch and see, the bird will trip!"
Nature trembles, a gentle quip.

The sunbeams cast their playful shade,
While chattering critters serenade.
"Let's play poker," says the spry old oak,
While vines entwine for an inside joke.

With every flutter, laughter reigns,
In leaves' embrace, all joy remains.
For in this quiet, comical tryst,
Nature's humor cannot be missed.

Nature's Ears Amidst the Branches

In the forest, whispers play,
Squirrels gossip night and day.
The owls wink and try to joke,
While bushes giggle, more than spoke.

Breezy chuckles through the pines,
As dancing ants mistake the lines.
A chipmunk nods, so wise and bright,
Says, "Who knew grass could take flight?"

Mossy rocks are old pranksters,
Offering glimpses of hidden monsters.
While rabbits tell of their new dreams,
And grasshoppers share their jumpy schemes.

The sunbeams chuckle on the way,
Spilling warmth, inviting play.
In nature's realm, a jest unfolds,
Where every story is funnier than told.

Murmurs Beneath the Bark

Beneath the bark, a chortle stirs,
Where beetles banter without spurs.
The mushrooms poke fun at clouds,
And giggling roots form silly crowds.

Now whispering twigs pass the word,
Of a prank where a tree was heard.
A woodpecker, with a tap and twirl,
Announces antics, watch that swirl!

The groundhog rolls his eyes in cheer,
While crickets clap from year to year.
With every rustle, a chuckle grows,
Nature's secrets in punchlines flows.

The ants are busy, marching loud,
Making jokes to entertain the crowd.
While the flowers sniff and sway in mirth,
Creating stories of joyful birth.

Conversations with the Shade

Among the shadows, secrets bloom,
Where lizards plot with perfect zoom.
A breeze crackles with puns on air,
While dandelions spin tales of flair.

The sunbeams peek, throw out a line,
As grass quips, declaring, "I'm fine!"
A gopher grins, waiting for a laugh,
While daisies dance in a silly graff.

The shade offers solace with a wink,
As mushrooms ponder, "What do we think?"
A mystery unfolds, with giggles abound,
In paths of laughter where fun is found.

The breezes tease with gentle touch,
Quaking limbs that laugh so much.
Every shade holds tales so bright,
Filling the day with sheer delight.

Treetop Tales of the Wind

Up high, the wind begins to twirl,
With trees that giggle in a swirl.
A parrot dives into the chat,
While squirrels wear the quirkiest hat.

The clouds above can hardly cope,
As sunbeams beam with endless hope.
Chasing shadows, a lighthearted race,
The branches sway with rhythmic grace.

The chattering leaves in joyous fife,
Share secrets of a tree's old life.
With every gust, a story spins,
Of playful sprites and cheeky sins.

In treetop realms, where laughter's brewed,
Each rustle brings a jovial mood.
So gather round, let's hear it all,
Nature's humor, ready to enthrall!

Resonance in the Grove

In the grove where whispers play,
Trees gossip at the end of the day.
Squirrels chuckle, branches sway,
Nature's jokes come out to stay.

A crow cracks wise, so bright and bold,
While acorns drop, a tale retold.
Rabbits giggle, their secrets unfold,
With every rustle, more fun controlled.

The robins chirp a funny tune,
As shadows shift beneath the moon.
A raccoon rants in a silly swoon,
While crickets dance, oh what a boon!

In this grove, the chatter's rife,
Each sound a spark, a punchy life.
Nature's humor, wild and rife,
Brings laughter through, this leafy strife.

Under the Whispering Stars

Under stars that gleam with glee,
The night sky's joke is plain to see.
Owls hoot puns, and crickets agree,
In cosmic laughter, we roam free.

Foxes trot with a cheeky grin,
While fireflies flash, oh, let's begin!
They dance like maniacs, all tuckered in,
Beneath the twinkling, starry din.

A raccoon snickers, he's got the plan,
Stealing snacks from a picnic can!
With every munch, he's living grand,
Nature's clowning—oh, isn't it bland?

In the moonlight's soft embrace,
We find ourselves in this silly space.
Where laughter drips at a gentle pace,
And joy ignites every face.

The Antiphony of Nature

Nature sings a duet bright,
Whimsical echoes in sheer delight.
The brook bubbles with pure insight,
While goats on cliffs giggle, what a sight!

Chirping frogs in an uproarious jest,
Compete with bees, who buzz with zest.
The wind starts howling with a snappy quest,
Bringing in laughter, nature's best!

In grassy fields where antics unfold,
Bunnies hop with humor bold.
A rustic waltz, their stories told,
Each leap a chuckle, never cold.

Nature's choir, with tones so grand,
Crafting mirth across the land.
In every note, we find our stand,
Laughing hearts, by fun, we're fanned.

Embracing the Atmospheric Whispers

In the breeze, silly stories weave,
As clouds burst forth, their jokes conceive.
The sun in strobe lights, what a reprieve,
Bringing humor that we believe!

A parrot squawks with vibrant flair,
While turtles tease, oh, it's quite rare!
The wind lets out a trumpeter's blare,
Encouraging fun in the open air.

The sky, a canvas, quirky and bright,
With rainbows that giggle—quite the sight!
Every sprinkle a joke, pure delight,
In nature's comedy, our hearts take flight.

So, let the whispers take their course,
And embrace the laughter, an endless force.
For in every twirl of nature's horse,
Lies a joyful heart, unbound, no remorse.

www.ingramcontent.com/pod-product-compliance
Lightning Source LLC
Chambersburg PA
CBHW072222070526
44585CB00015B/1455